Just Eat!

Collected by K-L Clinton and Stephanie Hutchinson

 NEW HOLLAND

the children's hospital at Westmead

Contents

Thank you • 4
Foreword • 5
Preface • 6

Soups & Snacks

David Atkins • Vegetable and Lamb Soup • 8
Nicky Buckley • Potato, Zucchini and Cheese Fritters • 10
Serge Dansereau • My Pea Soup • 12
Richard Glover • Homemade Elvis Pizza • 13
Belinda Green • Quick and Easy Pumpkin Soup • 16
Serge Dansereau • Father's Famous Baked Beans • 18
Antonia Kidman • Baby Lucia's Fine Lentil Soup • 20
Neil Perry • Asian Tea Eggs • 22
Joanna Savill • Simple Chinese Spring Rolls • 23
Jeanne Little • Scrambled Eggs, Bacon and Toast • 26
K-L Clinton • The Clinton Kids' San Choy Bau • 28
Heather Turland • Aussie Damper 30

Dinner's Done

Alyssa-Jane Cook • Mushroom and Spinach Quiche • 32
Bryce Courtenay • The World's Best Macaroni Cheese • 34
Gretel Killeen • Big Wally's Huge Fried Rice • 36
Lisa Curry and Grant Kenny • Mexican Beef 'n Bean Casserole • 38
Nova Peris-Kneebone • A-One Spaghetti Bolognese • 40
Rebel Penfold-Russell • Cauliflower and Potato Cheese • 42
Mick Doohan • Rissoles with Veg and Onion Gravy • 44
Greg Doyle • John Dory with Ginger Shallots • 46
Jeff Fenech • Meatballs and Tomato Sauce • 48
Lisa Ho • Hawaiian Chicken Schnitzels • 50
Wendy Heather Hunter • Delish Tuna and Pasta Dish • 52
Ita Buttrose • Cheese, Tomatoes and Chicken • 54

John Howard • Beef Burgundy • 56
Helen Kaminski • Homemade Cornish Pasties • 57
Elle Macpherson • Gran Fran's Beef and Veg Dish • 60
Nick Farr-Jones • Hale and Hearty Shepherd's Pie • 62
Tim Fischer • Greek Meatballs with Sauce • 64
Marcia Hines • Juicy Meatloaf • 66
Ken Done • Grilled Fish with Black Olives • 67
Iain Murray • Cheesy Chicken 'n Pasta Bake • 68
Stephen Price • Yummy Chicken and Veg Pie • 70
Anne Sargeant • Lamb Chops and Tomato Sauce • 72
John Laws • Cloud Valley Farm Pie • 74
Gai Waterhouse • Smoked Salmon Risotto • 76
Simone Young • Lemon Tarragon Chicken • 78
Stan Zemanek • Hamburgers with the Works • 80
Mark Taylor • Barbecued Steamed Fish • 82

Something Sweet

Kerry Chikarovski • My Nanna Coy's Butterfly Cakes • 84
Maureen Duval • Maureen's Very Easy Meringues • 86
Julian Gavin • Julian's Grand Hotcakes • 88
Midget Farrelly • Betty Farrelly's Dried Fruit Pie • 90
Gillian Armstrong • Peanut Butter Biscuits • 92
John Newcombe • Perfect Pecan Pie • 93
Serge Dansereau • Mother's Garden Fruit Crumble • 94
Johanna Griggs • Very Sticky Date Pudding • 96
Dick Smith • Golden Puffed Dumplings • 98
Monica Trapaga • Monica's Mum's Shortbread • 100
Mark Warren • Nutty Chocolate Brownies • 102
Lisa Wilkinson • Colourful Toffee Apple Treats • 104
John Bertrand • Fruit Dessert for the Family • 106
Peter Brock • Fruit Bread and Butter Custard • 108
Stephanie Hutchinson • Eily's Chocolate Cake • 110

...

Index • 112

Thank you

We have been overwhelmed by the enthusiasm generated by this book. In particular, it would never have been possible without the input of all our 'fabulous Aussies', who willingly gave us their favourite recipes and shared their parenting thoughts and inspirations with us. These Aussie cooks come from all walks of life—sports heroes, entertainers, artists, musicians, actors, fashion designers, models, politicians, restaurateurs and entrepreneurs—but regardless of how busy they were juggling work and family commitments, they all made the effort to contribute to *Just Eat!*

Foreword

The secrets of cancer cells are now being unlocked at The Children's Hospital at Westmead, thanks to the acquisition of leading edge technology—the latest Confocal Microscope Facility.

The confocal microscope is revolutionising the way that researchers look at living and non-living specimens—it will help unlock the structure of cells. This will significantly improve our understanding of the mechanisms that underpin cancer, which will lead to better identification of tumour types and improved diagnosis. Continued research into childhood cancer is vital in order to cure the one in four children who still sadly die from cancer, and so that we can make discoveries which will help everyone with cancer.

By buying this book, you have contributed to a donation that will help pay for and maintain the confocal microscope—vital equipment which allows researchers to embark on experiments that previously could only be dreamt about.

Finally, on behalf of all the children who will benefit from the research carried out in the Confocal Microscope Facility, I would like to thank all the celebrities who contributed to *Just Eat!*

Professor Peter Gunning
Oncology Research Unit
The Children's Hospital at Westmead

Preface

When a little girl in our neighbourhood lost her fight against leukaemia last year, it brought home to us just how precious our children are and how precious quality time together as a family is. It's easy to overlook the importance of families spending meal times together, sharing stories and learning about the day's ups and downs. And what could be more fun than preparing the meal together?

Just Eat! is a celebration of family mealtimes. To help us, we called on many well-known and much admired Australians, who willingly shared with us their favourite recipes. Tried and tested over the years, some of their recipes have been handed down from generation to generation and many are accompanied by inspirational messages. Kathy Lette even supplied us with the emergency recipe below for when time is really short!

Above all, we hope this cookbook brings families together—encouraging everyone to get back into the kitchen and have some fun, whether you are young or young at heart. And in the process we hope to raise funds for a very worthy cause—the Leukaemia Research and Support Fund—helping to improve the quality of life of Australia's most precious resource: our children.

K-L Clinton and Stephanie Hutchinson

Kathy Lette's Favourite Recipe

Motherhood offered me a whole new range of gastronomic angst. It took me ages to realise that a 'balanced' meal is whatever stays on the spoon en route to the baby's mouth. My kids have a favourite recipe that involves me dialling my finger to the bone. Just follow these simple steps:

1 • Pick up phone.
2 • Dial pizza place or local Chinese takeaway.
3 • Sit and gloat about how little washing-up you'll have to do later.

soups and snacks

Vegetable and

Never underestimate the power of logic in a child's mind.
One night, on our way home from a family outing, I was stopped
by the police for a random breath test. My two children,
Tobi and Joey, watched with interest as I blew very hard
into a little white tube and I think were quite relieved to see
that Dad was allowed to go on his way a free man!
The following morning, in the car on the way to school, little Joey
piped up from the back seat, ' Mum, how come that police lady
last night doesn' t realise that Daddy can already breathe?'

David aged four

DAVID ATKINS, PRODUCER, DIRECTOR, CHOREOGRAPHER

Lamb Soup

- 2 lamb necks
- 2 cups (350g) pearl barley
- salt and pepper
- 1 large brown onion
- 1 large swede
- 1 large turnip
- 2 large carrots
- 1 large parsnip
- 1 green pepper
- 2 sticks celery
- sprig parsley, finely chopped

1 • Cut all fat from lamb necks.
2 • Boil lamb necks with barley in plenty of salted water, until meat falls off the bone. Leave overnight or until fat settles.
3 • Skim off fat, remove bones and cut meat into bite-size pieces. Return meat to pot containing the liquid, with salt and pepper to taste.
4 • Cut all vegetables into dice-size pieces, or a little larger. Place in the pot with the meat, bring to the boil and reduce to a simmer until cooked.
5 • To serve, add a sprinkling of parsley to each bowl of soup.

SERVES FOUR

Potato, Zucchini

No matter what levels the kids push us to during the day, at night—when they're asleep—they're little angels.

Nicky aged five

NICKY BUCKLEY, TELEVISION PERSONALITY

& Cheese Fritters

- 2 medium potatoes, grated
- 2 medium zucchini, grated
- ½ cup (60g) grated cheddar cheese
- 2 eggs, lightly beaten
- pinch of ground nutmeg
- salt and pepper
- 2 tablespoons vegetable oil
- 25g margarine

1 • Coarsely grate potatoes and zucchini, then drain to remove as much liquid as possible.
2 • Place in a bowl and add grated cheese, eggs and seasoning.
3 • Heat oil and margarine in a frying pan.
4 • Form vegetable mixture into round, flat cakes and cook in the frying pan over a medium heat, turning frequently to brown both sides.

SERVES FOUR

My Pea Soup

Where I come from in the French part of Canada we eat lots of pea soup. Most pea soups are made with dry green peas, but I like my pea soup lighter and greener as it suits the Australian climate better. I serve it in my restaurant and it is very popular.

- 4 shallots, chopped
- 2 cloves garlic, chopped
- 1 small potato, chopped
- ½ leek, chopped
- 100g unsalted butter
- 6 cups (1½ litres) vegetable stock
- 500g peas
- 2 stalks mint
- ⅓ cup (100ml) fresh cream
- mint julienne (sliced mint leaves)

1. Heat the butter in a large pot, and sauté the vegetables (except the peas) until just starting to colour.
2. Add vegetable stock and simmer until the potatoes are cooked.
3. Add peas and mint stalks and simmer for one minute.
4. Pour into a container and allow to cool. When cold, purée the soup.
5. Whip the cream to soft peaks.
6. Heat the soup gently. When ready to serve, pour into a bowl, spoon on a small amount of cream and top with the mint julienne.

 SERVES SIX

SERGE DANSEREAU, CHEF

Homemade Elvis Pizza

We love cooking—despite the perpetual threat, for the adults in the family, of a diet. Here's the central problem: both our boys play soccer. The main means of fundraising is the sausage sizzle, held at every game and training session. Thus the cruel parenting irony: the fitter they get, the fatter we get. Frankly, I blame the kids!

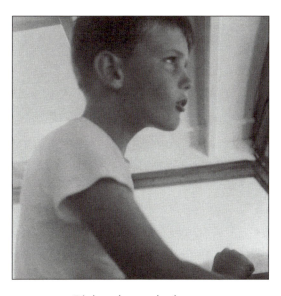

Richard aged eleven

Homemade Elvis Pizza

I'm a big Elvis fan, so this dish celebrates both the King's love of fast food, plus the shape of his best-selling LPs! Homemade pizza is great for Sunday tea, as you need time to let the dough rise. Even young kids can help chop up the toppings, and the older ones should have the strength to give the dough a good walloping. (Getting really good pizza involves kneading the dough for a full five minutes.)

Pizza base
- 1 sachet dried yeast
- ½ cup (125ml) warm water
- 1 tablespoon olive oil
- 1½ cups (185g) plain flour

Sauce
- 1 tablespoon olive oil
- 1 onion, chopped
- 1 clove garlic, finely chopped
- 425g can chopped tomatoes
- 1 teaspoon dried basil, or 1 tablespoon chopped fresh basil
- salt and pepper

Toppings
- 2 cups (240g) grated mozzarella cheese
- 1 cup (120g) chopped ham
- 1 cup (120g) chopped pineapple

1 • Dissolve yeast in the water, then stir in the olive oil.
2 • Place flour on your kitchen bench, making a little well in the middle, and pour in yeast mixture. Combine liquid with the flour, until you get a nice, pliable ball of dough, adding a little dry flour if necessary to stop it sticking.
3 • Flatten dough into the right shape with as many theatrical gestures as you dare, place on a lightly oiled tray, and leave for 45 minutes for the dough to rise.
4 • Preheat oven to 250°C. While you are waiting, prepare the sauce. First heat the oil in a saucepan, then add onion and garlic and fry until golden. Add tomatoes, basil, salt and pepper. Simmer away while your base is rising.
5 • When the pizza base is ready, cover the base with some mozzarella (the stuff in the pack will do), then a layer of the tomato sauce.
6 • Next, the children can add the toppings—they can decorate the bit of the pizza they have 'bagsed', or do one pizza each. We like ham and pineapple, but you could go sophisticated and use olives and salami.
7 • Put pizza in the oven and cook for 20 minutes.

 MAKES ONE PIZZA

Quick and Easy

*Lots of kids hate pumpkin, but my kids love my pumpkin soup.
I do everything by guesswork when it comes to quantities—
so good luck! I remember when my daughter Sally was six years
old we had a gathering of people at our place and Sally
announced, 'Stay for dinner! There are plenty of chairs'.
I didn't know what I was supposed to feed them all!
This meal would be perfect for unexpected extras.*

Belinda aged sixteen

BELINDA GREEN, TELEVISION PERSONALITY

Pumpkin Soup

- 2 tablespoons butter
- ¼ pumpkin, roughly chopped
- 2 teaspoons brown sugar
- 1 whole onion
- 3 cloves
- 500ml carton chicken stock
- 1 tablespoon milk or cream
- salt and pepper
- pinch nutmeg

1. Melt butter in a large pot and add pumpkin.
2. Sprinkle with brown sugar. Cook pumpkin until golden brown.
3. Stick the cloves into the onion (this gives it a great flavour). Add chicken stock and onion to pumpkin. Bring to the boil, then simmer until pumpkin is soft.
4. Remove from heat and blend until smooth. Add milk, a little salt and pepper and nutmeg.
5. Serve with crusty bread. Yum!

 SERVES FOUR

Father's Famous

My father was famous in the neighbourhood for his baked beans. He first showed me how to cook them properly on a fishing trip. After cooking our dinner of fish on the beach, he used the very warm sand to cover the pot of prepared beans and left them there overnight to cook slowly. In the morning when we woke up, we dug the pot out of the still hot sand and feasted on these delicious baked beans.

SERGE DANSEREAU, CHEF

Baked Beans

- 750g dry cannellini beans
- 1 onion, sliced
- 50ml molasses
- 150g brown sugar
- 1 tablespoon dry English mustard
- 150ml tomato sauce
- salt and pepper
- 1 bay leaf
- 100g salted pork flank (optional)

1 • Soak beans overnight in plenty of cold water to soften them.
2 • Drain away the water when ready to prepare the baked beans and rinse under cold water to remove any sand or grit.
3 • In a large pot, simmer the beans in plenty of water with a touch of salt until they start splitting. Skim the surface regularly, and add water if the level falls below the beans. Drain and retain your cooking liquid.
4 • Cool for one hour so as not to break the beans—they will be quite soft after cooking.
5 • Add the onion, molasses, brown sugar, mustard, tomato sauce and cooking liquid. Season lightly with the salt and pepper and add the bay leaf. To make more traditional baked beans, add a chunk of salted pork flank or bacon, and ideally you should use an earthenware or cast iron pot to bake the beans.
6 • Bake for 12 hours at 110°C, or overnight—it is best done overnight, just check in the morning to see if you need to add a touch of liquid.

SERVES FOUR

Baby Lucia's Fine

I give this to my baby, Lucia, who loves it. I find there is no need to purée it, but you can if you prefer. It's such a yummy soup that once I've made it I set aside Lucia's portion and add some chilli for the grown-ups. You can substitute any of the vegetables depending on what you have in the kitchen—pumpkin, celery and capsicum are all tasty alternatives.

Antonia aged ten

Lentil Soup

- 1 tablespoon olive oil
- 1 onion, chopped
- 1 carrot, chopped
- 1 small parsnip, chopped
- 1 potato, chopped
- $1^{1}/_{4}$ cups (230g) lentils
- 2 cups (500ml) chicken stock
- 1 cup (250ml) water
- bunch of broccoli, cut into florets
- 1 zucchini, chopped
- 275g can corn kernels

1 • In a heavy-based deep pan, cook the onion in olive oil until golden.
2 • Add carrot, parsnip and potato and cook for a few minutes longer.
3 • Add lentils, stock and water and bring to the boil.
4 • Add broccoli, zucchini and corn kernels and allow to simmer for approximately 45 minutes, or until the lentils are soft.

 Serves four

Asian Tea Eggs

A simple bowl of tea eggs is a thing of great beauty; the porcelain-like egg white crazed with the pattern of black tea. I love these little snacks with a bowl of rice, some Szechwan pickled cucumber and soy sauce or chilli oil. They are also a great building block in a sort of Asian antipasto. These are so easy—if you can boil water, you can make them!

- 6 free range eggs
- 3 tablespoons black tea
- 2 sticks cassia bark
- 3 whole star anise
- ½ teaspoon salt
- 5 tablespoons dark soy sauce

1 • Put the eggs in a small pan, cover with water and bring to the boil. Simmer for 10 minutes, then drain and plunge into iced water.
2 • Tap the eggs gently with the back of a spoon until covered all over with small cracks.
3 • Return the eggs to the pot and cover with fresh water.
4 • Add the tea, cassia bark, star anise, salt and soy sauce.
5 • Simmer gently for one hour, remove from the heat and leave in the stock until cool.
6 • Take the eggs out of the stock, remove the shells and serve in a simple bowl.

MAKES SIX EGGS

Simple Chinese Spring Rolls

These are very popular with my two daughters, Lily Rose and Milena. You can involve children in making them—they are pretty easy to roll and the odd wobbly parcel is actually not a problem, as long as all the filling stays in. You can also hide vaguely healthy things in a nice crunchy exterior, so that bits of green and orange stuff like Chinese spinach and carrot, even celery and water chestnuts, go largely unnoticed.

Joanna (aged two) and family

TELEVISION PRESENTER, JOANNA SAVILL

Simple Chinese Spring Rolls

- ½ packet rice vermicelli
- 1 tablespoon oil
- 3 stalks spring onions, finely diced
- 1 carrot, finely chopped
- 1 stick celery, finely diced
- 3 water chestnuts, finely diced (optional)
- 3 stalks Chinese spinach (gai larn), finely shredded
- 1 clove garlic, minced
- 1 small knob fresh ginger, minced
- 100g pork mince
- 100g chicken mince
- splash of light soy sauce
- drizzle dark sweet soy sauce (kecap manis)
- 2 teaspoons cornflour
- ¼ cup (60ml) chicken stock or water
- 1 packet frozen spring roll wrappers (about 20), defrosted
- peanut or olive oil, for deep frying

1. Blanch rice vermicelli in boiling water for two minutes (or according to instructions on packet). Strain and run immediately under cold water. Leave to drain.
2. Heat half the oil in a wok and stir-fry spring onions, carrot, celery and water chestnuts for a few minutes until soft. Add Chinese spinach and allow to wilt. Remove vegetables from the wok and set aside.

3 • Using the remaining oil, fry garlic and ginger for about one minute, then add mince and cook until lightly browned. Season with soy sauces and cook for another couple of minutes.

4 • Add a little water or chicken stock to the cornflour to make a paste and stir into the mince mixture, cooking for about one more minute. This will slightly thicken the filling.

5 • Return vegetables to the wok and stir through. Turn off the heat and add the rice vermicelli, stirring gently but well. Allow the filling to cool.

6 • Lay out a spring roll wrapper in a diamond shape in front of you. Place 2 tablespoons of mixture in the centre of the bottom half, about 3cm from the corner closest to you and leaving about 3cm on each side. Fold the bottom corner over the mixture and keep rolling away from you until half the wrapper has been rolled up. At this point fold in the sides and keep rolling to the end. Seal the last edge by dipping your finger into a little warm water and moistening the final flap.

7 • Heat oil in a wok and when it's spitting hot (don't involve the kids in this part) drop one roll in to test. Lightly and quickly brown it on both sides. Gradually add the remaining rolls. Remove and drain them as you go on absorbent paper.

8 • Serve with a ready-made sweet and sour dipping sauce or a little light soy sauce, which I always dilute with a little water or chicken stock to stop the kids getting too much of a salty soy hit.

SERVES FOUR

Scrambled Eggs,

This is an easy recipe for small children to make for Mum or Dad when it's a special day, to serve in bed. Set a tray with knife, fork, salt and pepper, a serviette and a flower from your garden (or a neighbour's if you haven't got a garden!).

JEANNE LITTLE, TELEVISION PERSONALITY

Bacon and Toast

- 1 tablespoon butter or oil
- 2 rashers bacon
- 2 slices bread
- 3 eggs
- salt and pepper
- 2 tablespoons cold water
- butter

1. Grease a frying pan with butter or oil.
2. Flatten the bacon on a board, cut off most of the fat around the edge, and run your finger over the meat. If there are any 'bones' (little hard bits) cut them out.
3. Turn on a hotplate, underneath the frying pan, to low–medium heat. Put bacon into the pan to cook, turning when brown on one side.
4. Put bread into the toaster to cook.
5. Crack the eggs into a bowl, beat with a fork, add a pinch of salt, a good amount of black pepper and the cold water. Beat again.
6. When the bacon is ready, place on kitchen paper to drain.
7. Add some more butter to the pan, pour in the eggs and when still runny, give a quick stir with a fork. Don't overcook or they will go dry.
8. Serve the bacon and eggs on a warm plate (you can warm it under a hot tap, but don't forget to dry it!) and place a sprig of parsley on the eggs. Place toast that has been buttered on the side of the plate and serve!

SERVES ONE

The Clinton Kids'

*This is a hit with my five kids—
it is a healthy, fuss free, winner of a dinner!*

K-L's kids: Max, Jack, Tom, Bella
and India Clinton

San Choy Bau

- 1 Iceberg lettuce
- 1 tablespoon soy sauce
- 1 tablespoon oyster sauce
- 2 teaspoons hoi sin sauce
- ½ cup (125ml) chicken stock
- 1 teaspoon sugar
- 2 teaspoons cornflour
- 2–3 tablespoons of olive oil
- 2 cloves garlic, chopped
- 500g beef, chicken or pork mince
- 1 tablespoon chopped coriander
- 2 cups chopped vegetables, e.g. snow peas, corn, peas, capsicum, bean shoots
- 3 shallots, chopped
- sprinkle of pine nuts (optional)

1. Remove outer leaves of lettuce, retaining the smaller cup-shaped leaves. Keep the kids busy, let them trim the leaves and put in a bowl of iced water (the leaves will still work without doing this if you run out of time).
2. Mix sauces, stock, sugar and cornflour in a small bowl, stirring until the cornflour is dissolved. Set aside.
3. Heat oil in a wok or frying pan, add garlic and cook briefly over a high heat. Add the mince, breaking up any lumps, and the coriander and shallots.
4. Pour in the sauce mixture and stir until it boils and thickens, which takes one to two minutes.
5. Add vegetables and pine nuts.
6. Place drained lettuce cups on a plate and spoon in the filling. No need for forks or chopsticks, hands are perfect for the job!

Aussie Damper

We are the moulders and creators of our future generation, instilling love, happiness, confidence and self esteem in the hearts of our children. Then we give them wings to fly. This is the true meaning of success and every parent's dream.

- 3 cups (375g) self-raising flour
- 1–2 teaspoons salt
- ½ cup (90g) butter
- ½ cup (125ml) milk
- ½ cup (125ml) water
- a little extra milk and flour

1. Preheat oven to 210°C and grease a baking tray.
2. Sift the flour and salt into a large bowl and make a little well in the centre.
3. Mix the butter, milk and water and add it slowly to the flour. Stir until just combined.
4. Place on a lightly floured surface and knead until smooth.
5. Place the dough onto the tray and press out to a 20cm round.
6. Score the damper into triangular sections with the tip of a knife, with cuts 1cm deep.
7. Brush with a little extra milk to glaze and dust with flour.
8. Bake for 10 minutes and then reduce the heat to 180°C and cook for another 15 minutes, or until the bread is a golden brown colour.
9. Serve hot with butter and your favourite toppings.

 MAKES ONE LOAF

dinner's done

ALYSSA-JANE COOK, ACTRESS

Mushroom and

This is a delicious and simple dish, which my daughters love to eat. You can also substitute salmon, lemon rind and dill for spinach and mushrooms. Enjoy!

Alyssa-Jane aged six with her little sister

Spinach Quiche

- 1 prepared 25 cm pastry case
- 1 bunch English spinach
- 1 onion
- 1 cup (200g) chopped mushrooms
- 1 tablespoon olive oil
- 1 cup (250ml) ricotta or cream cheese
- 1 cup (120g) grated cheddar cheese
- 5 eggs
- 2/3 cup (160ml) sour cream
- 1 teaspoon ground nutmeg
- salt and pepper

1 • Preheat oven to 180°C.
2 • Plunge spinach leaves into boiling water for one minute, rinse and drain well.
3 • Sauté onion and mushrooms in oil until soft. Allow to cool.
4 • Shred spinach and place in a bowl. Add ricotta cheese, grated cheese, eggs, sour cream, nutmeg and sautéed onions and mushrooms. Season with salt and pepper.
5 • Pour filling into pastry case and bake for 35 minutes, or until lightly browned on top.

SERVES SIX

The World's Best

It may interest you to know that I probably make the best macaroni cheese in the history of the world. Though vegetarian entirely, it is not without an overabundant whack of calories—the sort of dish served to hungry teenagers after a game of football.

- 500g packet macaroni
- 1½ kg tasty cheddar
- 1 onion
- 3 tomatoes
- 200g can peas
- 2 eggs
- 2 cups (500ml) milk
- 2 tablespoons tomato purée
- 1 teaspoon Keen's mustard powder
- black pepper

Macaroni Cheese

1. Cook macaroni in plenty of boiling, salted water. Rinse thoroughly and allow to cool. Preheat oven to 180°C.
2. Grate cheese and put aside for layering. Chop onion and slice tomatoes. Drain peas from juice and discard juice.
3. Break eggs into a bowl, add milk and tomato purée and beat thoroughly until well combined.
4. In a deep casserole or pan, add a layer of macaroni (about 2cm depth). Add an equal layer of cheese and a layer of tomatoes, coarse pepper and the mustard powder.
5. Add another layer of macaroni and sprinkle liberally with peas.
6. Add a layer of cheese and sprinkle liberally with onion.
7. Add another layer of macaroni, followed by a layer of tomatoes and peas, then more cheese sprinkled with onion.
8. Add a fourth layer of macaroni then pour on the egg mixture so that the entire dish is soaked through. Finally, add a double layer of cheese.
9. Bake in the oven for 40 minutes until cheese is well browned on top. Serve piping hot and claim your hero status in the family.

SERVES EIGHT

GRETEL KILLEEN, JOURNALIST AND AUTHOR

Big Wally's Huge

*Never tell your children that the food you've prepared is actually healthy and good for them. Always tell them that the food is 'rubbish', that it will rot their teeth and stunt their growth and slowly but surely eat up their gizzards.
That way they'll beg you for seconds!*

Gretel aged nine

Fried Rice

- 2¼ cups (470g) white rice
- dash of butter
- 1 tablespoon olive oil
- 1 large white onion, chopped
- 4 rashers bacon, chopped and rind removed
- ½ red capsicum, chopped
- ½ green capsicum, chopped
- ½ cup (75g) frozen peas
- ½ cup (75g) frozen prawns
- 3 eggs, beaten
- 1 tablespoon soy sauce

1. Add rice and butter to a saucepan of boiling, salted water. Cook for 12 minutes, stirring regularly.
2. When rice is cooked, place in a colander to drain then run under hot water. (If at this stage the rice is 'gluggy' seize the opportunity to tell everyone that you're making a risotto).
3. In a pan or wok, heat oil and fry onion, bacon, capsicum, peas and prawns (plus any leftovers that you have, e.g. barbecued chicken, leftover roast beef, ham, celery etc.)
4. When just about cooked add peas.
5. Pour beaten eggs into the pan and stir well into the ingredients to cook the eggs.
6. Add rice and stir, adding soy sauce to flavour.

SERVES FOUR

Mexican Beef 'n

Before cooking, remember to remove the instructions from your oven! Grant and I moved into our first house and we couldn't find any instructions for the oven. One night I was grilling some chops and suddenly huge flames started leaping out of the griller and nearly burnt down the entire kitchen — after we put the fire out we discovered that the oven instructions were under the tray in the griller! Happy cooking!

LISA CURRY AND GRANT KENNY, SPORTS PERSONALITIES

Bean Casserole

- 1 tablespoon oil
- 1 onion, finely chopped
- 500g lean minced beef
- 2 cloves garlic, finely chopped
- 1 teaspoon chilli powder
- 2 tablespoons tomato paste
- 425g can whole peeled tomatoes
- 300g can red kidney beans
- 1 packet taco seasoning
- 200g low-fat cottage cheese
- 1¼ cups (300ml) lite sour cream
- 1 packet corn chips
- 3 cups (330g) grated low-fat cheddar cheese
- 1 tablespoon paprika

1. Preheat oven to 180°C.
2. Heat oil in a frying pan over a medium heat. Add onion and cook until soft and golden. Add mince, garlic, chilli powder, tomato paste, tomatoes, beans and taco seasoning and cook until mince is brown. Reduce heat and simmer for 20 minutes.
3. Place a layer of mince on the bottom of a casserole dish. Smooth over a layer of cottage cheese and sour cream and then a layer of corn chips and grated cheese. Continue to layer all ingredients in this order and finish off with a layer of mince on top.
4. Cover with layer of corn chips and sprinkle with grated cheese and paprika.
5. Bake in the oven for approximately five to eight minutes or until the cheese melts on top.

 SERVES SIX

A-One Spaghetti

I scored an 'A' for this recipe when it was handed in as an assignment for the Year 10 class cookbook at Dripstone High School, 1985!

Nova aged eight

NOVA PERIS-KNEEBONE, ATHLETE

Bolognese

- ½ onion, chopped
- 1 clove garlic, crushed
- 2 tablespoons oil
- 200g minced beef
- 1 tomato, finely diced
- ¼ cup (60ml) water
- 1 tablespoon tomato paste
- 1 tablespoon salt
- ½ tablespoon crushed pepper
- ½ tablespoon mixed herbs
- 100g spaghetti
- 2 tablespoons grated cheddar cheese

1 • Fry onion and garlic in oil until light brown.
2 • Add mince and fry lightly, stirring to break up any lumps.
3 • Add tomato, tomato paste, water, salt, pepper and herbs, stir and simmer, covered, for 30 minutes.
4 • Cook spaghetti in 3 cups (750ml) boiling water for 15 minutes or until tender.
5 • Drain spaghetti and keep warm.
6 • Serve spaghetti with meat sauce on top and sprinkle with cheese.

SERVES FOUR

Cauliflower and

REBEL PENFOLD-RUSSELL, FILM PRODUCER

Children: entertain, educate, empower.

Rebel aged four

Potato Cheese

- 2 large organic potatoes
- ½ organic cauliflower
- 1 tablespoon butter
- 2 tablespoons plain flour
- ¼ cup (60ml) milk
- 1 cup (120g) grated non-rennet cheese (available at the health food store)
- 3 tablespoons chopped parsley (home-grown if possible!)
- 2 tablespoons chopped chives
- cracked pepper and salt

1. Preheat oven to 180°C.
2. Slice potatoes and cauliflower thinly and place in a baking dish. (You can soften them first by cooking in the microwave for three minutes.)
3. Melt butter in a saucepan and sprinkle in the flour to make a roux.
4. Gradually add milk, cheese, herbs, pepper and salt, stirring until the sauce is thick and creamy.
5. Spread the sauce over cauliflower and potatoes and bake in the oven for 20 minutes.
6. Leftovers of cauliflower cheese can be puréed, mixed with rice, a beaten organic egg and rolled in a seaweed mixture called nori komi furikake (available from health food or Japanese stores). Alternatively, this is an excellent mixture for sprinkling on salads or steamed sushi rice.

 SERVES FOUR

Rissoles with Veg

Children: a moment to enjoy and a time to remember.

Rissoles
- 1 kg minced beef
- 1 carrot, finely diced
- 1 onion, finely diced
- ½ cup (30g) breadcrumbs
- 3 eggs
- 3 teaspoons Worcestershire sauce
- 3 teaspoons all purpose seasoning
- salt and pepper
- 2 tablespoons chopped fresh parsley
- 3 tablespoons plain flour
- 3 teaspoons peanut or olive oil

Mashed potato
- 5 large potatoes
- 1 tablespoon butter
- ½ cup (125ml) milk
- salt and pepper

Mint peas
- 500g frozen or fresh peas
- 2 tablespoons chopped fresh mint

Onion gravy
- 2 large onions, chopped
- 1 tablespoon butter
- 2 cloves garlic, finely chopped
- 1 cup (250ml) beef stock
- 2 teaspoons cornflour
- 1 tablespoon cold water
- salt and pepper

and Onion Gravy

1. Mix all the ingredients for rissoles (except flour and oil) together in a large bowl.
2. Roll into round portions, using the palms of your hand, and dust in the flour.
3. Pan fry rissoles in oil, and keep warm.
4. Peel potatoes and boil until soft. When cooked, drain and mash with remaining ingredients and keep warm.
5. While potatoes are cooking, boil peas for 10 minutes. Add mint to peas after five minutes, strain and keep warm.
6. To make the gravy, pan fry onions in butter until golden brown. Add chopped garlic and cook for one minute.
7. Add stock and cook for a further five minutes on low heat.
8. Mix cornflour with cold water and add to gravy, stirring until it thickens. Season to taste with salt and pepper.
9. Serve rissoles and mashed potatoes with mint peas on the side, and pour over the gravy.

SERVES EIGHT

John Dory with

A famous French chef once quoted, 'I like to start the day with a glass of champagne. I like to finish it with champagne. To be frank, I also like a glass or two in between...' Not a bad tip for frazzled parents — take 1–2 cups as needed!

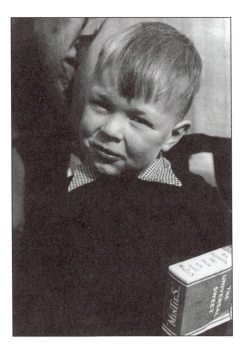

Greg aged three

GREG DOYLE, CHEF

Ginger Shallots

- 4 tablespoons butter
- 1 knob fresh ginger, thinly sliced
- 4 shallots, cut into 3cm strips
- 2 x 600g whole John Dory, or 4 fillets
- 1 cup (250ml) fresh fish stock
- salt and pepper

1 • Preheat oven to 200°C.
2 • Heat butter in a shallow, ovenproof pan. Add ginger and shallots and stir.
3 • Season fish with salt and pepper and add to pan. Add fish stock and cover with a lid.
4 • Place in the oven and cook for approximately eight minutes.
5 • Remove pan from oven and remove the fish onto serving plates.
6 • Heat sauce remaining in pan and bring to the boil. Spoon over the fish and serve.

 SERVES TWO

Meatballs and

As a parent I learnt how important it is to teach my kids to respect others, because at the end of the day, whether you are rich or poor, black or white, we are all the same.
Here is my children's favourite recipe. Have yourself a good meal!

Jeff aged fifteen

JEFF FENECH, WORLD BOXING CHAMPION

Tomato Sauce

SAUCE
- 1 tablespoon vegetable oil
- 1 onion, chopped
- 425g can chopped tomatoes
- salt and pepper

MEATBALLS
- 500g lean minced beef
- ½ cup (30g) breadcrumbs
- 1 egg
- 2 garlic cloves, finely chopped
- 1 onion
- 2 tablespoons freshly grated parmesan cheese
- salt and pepper
- 1 tablespoon vegetable oil

1. To make the sauce, heat oil and chopped onions in a pan and cook until soft.
2. Pour in tomatoes and add a little salt and pepper. Keep simmering until ready to use.
3. Combine mince with breadcrumbs, egg, garlic, onion, parmesan, salt and pepper. Using your hands, roll the mixture into medium-sized balls.
4. Fry balls in oil until browned, then remove and drain well, add to tomato sauce and cook for a further 40 minutes.
5. Serve with mashed potato.

 **SERVES FOUR**

Hawaiian Chicken

Treat your children as your equals, but still keep the fantasy.

- 500g fresh chicken thigh fillets
- 1 teaspoon sesame oil
- 1 teaspoon soy sauce
- 1 teaspoon dry dill tips
- ½ tablespoon plain flour, plus extra for dipping
- 1 egg
- 1 cup (250ml) cold water
- 1 cup (60g) breadcrumbs
- 1 cup (250ml) sweet and sour sauce
- 2 slices pineapple, very thinly sliced
- 1 teaspoon chopped fresh ginger
- ½ onion, very thinly sliced
- peanut or olive oil for frying

LISA HO, FASHION DESIGNER

Schnitzels

1. Remove all fat from the chicken and score the flesh.
2. Season with a few drops of sesame oil, soy sauce and sprinkle with dry dill tips. Mix and let stand in the refrigerator.
3. Mix the flour, egg and water to make a batter.
4. Dip the chicken fillets into some flour (this gives the chicken a crunchier finish), then dip in the batter, and drop into a flat dish of breadcrumbs. Cover fillets with breadcrumbs then push down to flatten. Shake off any excess breadcrumbs and put aside.
5. Gently warm the sweet and sour sauce and add pineapple, ginger and onion.
6. Fry chicken fillets in oil at a high temperature and cook until golden.
7. Slice the fillets and arrange on a bed of steamed rice with the sauce over the top.

SERVES FOUR

Delish Tuna and

'Too many cooks spoil the broth' doesn't apply to kids, because they love to cook!

Wendy aged three

WENDY HEATHER HUNTER, FASHION DESIGNER

Pasta Dish

- ¼ cup (45g) butter
- 2 tablespoons plain flour
- 1½ cups (375ml) milk
- 425g can tuna, drained
- 2 cups cooked pasta
- 1¾ cups (210g) grated tasty cheese
- chopped parsley, to serve

1. Melt butter in a medium-sized, heavy-based pan.
2. Remove from heat, stir in flour and return to the heat for one to two minutes.
3. Remove pan from heat again and gradually stir in the milk.
4. Return sauce to the heat. Stir constantly over a medium heat until the mixture boils and thickens.
5. Remove from heat and stir in tuna, pasta and 1 cup grated cheese.
6. Spoon mixture into a greased heatproof dish and top with the remaining cheese.
7. Put under a preheated hot grill for one to two minutes, or until the cheese has melted.
8. Top with chopped parsley just before serving.

SERVES FOUR

Cheese, Tomatoes

My kids, like all kids I suspect, loved eating simple dishes like roast chicken and chips; spaghetti bolognese; and roast lamb with baked spuds, pumpkin, peas and gravy. I don't believe you should ever force kids to eat. If they don't want to eat vegetables when they're little don't fret—if they are well and healthy they'll make up their own minds on when to include vegetables in their diet! One of my kids' favourite dishes was chicken, tomatoes and cheese with mashed potatoes. It's a very easy dish to make—and very delicious!

and Chicken

- 500g chicken breast fillets, or chicken thigh fillets
- 1 tablespoon olive oil
- 1 clove garlic, finely chopped
- 2 fresh tomatoes, diced
- 3 tablespoons tomato purée
- 1 ¼ cups (150g) grated cheese (we used a combination of cheddar and parmesan)

1 • Over a low heat, gently cook chicken and garlic in a pan with the olive oil.

2 • When chicken is almost cooked, cover with diced tomatoes and add tomato purée.

3 • Add grated cheese and keep simmering. (The cheese will melt and the sauce will thicken.)

4 • Serve with mashed potatoes. My kids loved this dish with fresh peas, too. You can substitute veal steaks for the chicken for an even more special dinner and serve with a lettuce and cucumber salad.

SERVES FOUR

Beef Burgundy

This recipe works best if cooked in the one pot at all stages, preferably a cast iron casserole pot.

- 1kg beef (blade or chuck, with fat and gristle removed)
- 1 tablespoon olive oil
- 1 large onion, chopped
- 1 clove garlic, finely chopped
- 1 cup (200g) button mushrooms
- 1 teaspoon dried basil
- salt and pepper
- 1 cup (250ml) red wine (or 425g can tinned tomatoes, if preferred)

1 • Preheat oven to 170°C.
2 • Cut meat into large cubes.
3 • Heat cooking pot on top of stove and add olive oil.
4 • Gently cook onion and garlic until golden.
5 • Add meat and cook until browned.
6 • Add mushrooms, basil, salt, pepper and wine (or tomatoes).
7 • Put lid on pot and place in the oven for 1½ hours.
8 • Serve with plain rice, tagliatelle or potatoes.

SERVES EIGHT

Homemade Cornish Pasties

Don't listen to 'you'll make a rod for your own back' comments. Spoil children with love. They get to be easier and better company as the years go by. For them life only gets harder and they might as well have it all while they think this is the way it is!

Helen (back row) and friends

DESIGNER, HELEN KAMINSKI

Homemade Cornish Pasties

PASTRY
- 2 tablespoons butter
- 5 tablespoons plain flour
- salt and pepper
- 4 tablespoons water

FILLING
- 200g skirt steak, finely sliced across the grain
- 1 swede, cut into small dice
- 2 large potatoes, cut into small dice
- 1 onion, cut into small dice
- 1 carrot, cut into small dice
- salt and pepper
- knob of butter
- 4 teaspoons hot water

1. To make the pastry, place butter, flour, salt and pepper into a blender and mix until it looks like crumbs (a few seconds).
2. Add cold water slowly until it suddenly balls up into a solid mass. This will make an easy to handle pastry that is not very rich. (Add more butter for a richer, more tender and crumbling pastry. Alternatively, add cold milk instead of water for more richness.)

3 • Wrap in plastic and leave in the refrigerator for half-an-hour to settle before rolling. Preheat the oven to 180°C.

4 • Roll out pastry into ovals approximately 20cm x 12cm. Place a little of the raw meat and vegetables in an oval pile in the centre of the pastry, leaving enough area around the outside of the pile to draw up the pastry into a rolled and pinched seam over the top. (The trick is not to over-fill the pastry. If you do you will have trouble closing it.) Season meat and vegetables with salt and pepper.

5 • Dampen the outside area of the pastry very lightly with fingers dipped in water. (This will allow the pastry to bond better while you close the edges together.) Starting at the top of the pastry oval, begin to close and twist the pastry, rolling the edges very slightly as you go and pinching them together.

6 • Place pasties on a baking tray, prick once with a fork and cook in the oven until lightly browned.

7 • As soon as the pasties are cooked, remove from oven and, with a spoon, break open a small hole in the top and push in a knob of butter and a teaspoon of hot water. This will give a little richness to the lean skirt steak.

8 • Serve hot—probably with tomato sauce for the kids!

SERVES FOUR (MAKES 6–8 PASTIES)

Gran Fran's Beef

This recipe originated from my mother, Fran Macpherson, and is the same one that she prepared for me, Mimi, Ben and Elizabeth. Arki and I both love this as much as Flynn— so it is always made in double quantity!

Elle aged eight

ELLE MACPHERSON, MODEL

and Veg Dish

- 1 onion, chopped
- 500g lean minced beef
- 1 tablespoon vegemite
- 1 teaspoon HP sauce
- 1 tablespoon tomato sauce
- 1 tablespoon Worcestershire sauce
- 3 carrots, chopped
- 2 potatoes, chopped
- 1 bunch broccoli, cut into florets
- 1 cup (200g) peas, fresh or frozen

1. Add onion and meat to a large pan and cook, stirring, over a high heat until the meat is brown.
2. Add vegemite, HP sauce, tomato sauce and Worcestershire sauce.
3. Lightly steam carrots, potatoes and broccoli.
4. Add vegetables and peas to meat.
5. Add lots of love, and simmer until cooked!

SERVES FOUR

Hale and Hearty

This is a great way to give kids lots of vegetables without them knowing it!

- 1 tablespoon olive oil
- 1 large onion, thinly sliced
- 2 cloves garlic, crushed
- 500g lean minced beef
- 2 large tomatoes, peeled and chopped
- 1 large carrot, grated
- 1 small zucchini, grated
- 2 tablespoons tomato sauce
- 2 tablespoons Worcestershire sauce
- 4 large potatoes, mashed
- ½ cup (60g) grated cheese

NICK FARR-JONES, FORMER WALLABIES CAPTAIN

Shepherd's Pie

1. Heat oil in a pan, add onion and garlic. Cook on medium heat for one to two minutes.
2. Add mince and stir with a wooden spoon until the meat is well browned. Cover and cook for 30 minutes. Preheat oven to moderate 180°C.
3. Add tomatoes, grated carrot and zucchini to mince.
4. Cook on a low heat for 30 minutes, then stir in the tomato and Worcestershire sauces.
5. Put mixture into an ovenproof dish, top with mashed potato and sprinkle with grated cheese.
6. Bake in the oven for 15 minutes or until cheese is melted and brown.

 SERVES FOUR

Greek Meatballs

These are no ordinary meatballs. With a hint of Mediterranean flavour, a simple dish is transformed. And the best thing is they are just as delicious cold, so any leftovers taste just as good the next day—that is if there are any leftovers!

Tim with his sons Harrison and Dominic

TIM FISCHER, POLITICIAN

with Sauce

MEATBALLS
- 500g lean minced beef
- ½ cup (30g) breadcrumbs
- 1 egg
- 1 onion, chopped
- 2 cloves garlic, chopped
- ½ teaspoon dried oregano
- ½ teaspoon cloves
- 1 tablespoon chopped fresh parsley
- 1 tablespoon chopped fresh mint
- squeeze lemon juice

SAUCE
- 400g can whole peeled tomatoes
- ¼ cup (60ml) water
- 1 teaspoon sugar
- salt and pepper

1. Preheat oven to 220°C.
2. To make meatballs, place all the ingredients into a bowl and mix thoroughly.
3. Take a small amount of the mixture, shape into a ball and place on a baking tray. Repeat with the remaining mixture.
4. Bake in the oven for approximately 20 minutes.
5. While the meatballs are cooking, purée tomatoes in a food processor and pour through a sieve to remove the seeds.
6. Place in a saucepan and add water, sugar, salt and pepper. Simmer for 15 minutes.
7. When the meatballs are cooked, pour over the sauce and serve.

 SERVES FOUR

Juicy Meatloaf

Take time out every day to listen to your children.

Meatloaf
- 1kg minced beef
- 1 cup (60g) fresh breadcrumbs
- 2 onions, finely diced
- 2 teaspoons curry powder
- 1 egg, lightly beaten
- ½ cup (125ml) milk
- ½ cup (125ml) water
- salt and pepper
- sprinkle of chopped parsley

Sauce
- ½ cup (125ml) water
- ½ cup (125ml) tomato sauce
- ¼ cup (60ml) Worcestershire sauce
- 1 tablespoon brown sugar
- 30g butter
- 2 tablespoons lemon juice

1. Preheat oven to 180°C.
2. Bring sauce ingredients to the boil in a saucepan and set aside.
3. Combine ingredients for meatloaf in a large bowl. Mix well and pour into a greased loaf tin.
4. Bake in the oven for 30 minutes.
5. Remove from oven and carefully pour off any excess fat.
6. Pour over the sauce and return to oven for a further 40 minutes.

 Serves eight

Marcia Hines, Singer

Grilled Fish with Black Olives

Give your kids lots and lots of love and a little bit of discipline when required.

- 2 tablespoons olive oil
- 1 tablespoon balsamic vinegar
- salt and pepper
- 2 fresh fish fillets, e.g. ling or perch
- 1 cup (155g) black olives
- 2 tablespoons chopped flat leaf parsley

1. Mix olive oil, vinegar, salt and pepper and baste each fillet with the dressing.
2. Grill on the first side until well-marked. Turn fish over gently and cook other side.
3. Mash olives (removing any pips) and add parsley.
4. Place the fish on a plate and surround it with the olive mixture.
5. Drizzle extra oil and vinegar over the top.
6. Serve with crusty bread and fresh, green salad.

 SERVES TWO

ARTIST, KEN DONE

Cheesy Chicken 'n

This is my favourite dinner, which my girls love to help me cook. It's easy to prepare and there are never any leftovers, which is always a good sign!

Iain aged six

Pasta Bake

- 350g shell pasta
- 2 tablespoons butter
- ½ onion, chopped
- 300g chicken fillets, sliced
- 3 tablespoons creamed cheese spread
- 1 cup (120g) grated cheese
- 1½ cups (375ml) milk
- ¼ cup (60ml) sour cream
- 1 teaspoon lemon juice
- salt and pepper
- ¼ cup (15g) breadcrumbs

1 • Preheat oven to 160°C. Boil pasta in salted water, until al dente.
2 • Melt butter in a saucepan and sauté onion for one minute.
3 • Add chicken and cook until golden brown. Remove from heat.
4 • Add cheese spread and half the grated cheese to butter and onion.
5 • Add milk and sour cream and stir on low heat until all ingredients have melted into a creamy sauce.
6 • Add lemon juice, salt and pepper and stir on low heat for five minutes. Do not boil.
7 • Place cooked pasta and chicken in a deep baking dish. Pour over the sauce and mix thoroughly.
8 • Combine breadcrumbs and remaining grated cheese and generously scatter on top.
9 • Place, uncovered, in a preheated 160°C oven for 30 minutes or until the top turns brown and crispy.

— SERVES SIX

Yummy Chicken

When I was younger, my mother used to tell me, 'Be your best'. This is something I will instil in my girls, as well as the children I meet when I visit schools. It is very simple but if everybody did it, the world would be a better place.

- 2 tablespoons butter
- 1 onion, chopped
- 1 celery stalk, chopped
- 1 carrot, sliced
- 2 tablespoons flour
- 1 cup (250ml) milk
- 1 teaspoon dried oregano
- 2 chicken stock cubes
- 2 cups (300g) diced chicken
- 310g can whole corn kernels, drained
- 2 sheets puff pastry
- beaten egg to glaze (optional)

and Veg Pie

1. Preheat oven to 200°C.
2. Heat butter in a saucepan. Add vegetables and cook for two minutes.
3. Stir in flour and cook, stirring, for a further minute.
4. Slowly stir in milk, oregano and stock cubes. Bring to the boil, stirring, and simmer over a low heat for two to three minutes. Keep stirring occasionally.
5. Remove from heat and cool, then stir in chicken and corn.
6. Line a pie dish with one pastry sheet. Add chicken mixture.
7. Place remaining pastry sheet over the top, pressing the edges together to seal, trimming off excess pastry.
8. Cut a slit in the centre of the pastry to allow the steam to escape. Brush pastry with beaten egg, if desired.
9. Bake in the oven for 40–45 minutes or until the pastry is golden brown and the chicken is thoroughly cooked.

SERVES SIX TO EIGHT

ANNE SARGEANT, FORMER NETBALL CAPTAIN

Lamb Chops and

Tell your kids you love them every day and don't forget to tell your parents the same thing!

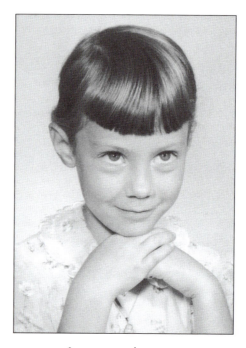

Anne aged seven

Tomato Sauce

- 1 tablespoon oil
- 1 onion, sliced
- 2 cloves garlic, crushed
- 8 lamb chump chops
- 470g can natural tomato soup
- ½ cup (125ml) milk
- 1 green capsicum, sliced
- 1 red capsicum, sliced
- 1 cup (200g) sliced mushrooms
- 425g can whole peeled tomatoes
- 2 teaspoons Worcestershire sauce
- 2 teaspoons soy sauce
- 2 teaspoons dried basil
- salt and pepper
- 8 new potatoes, par-boiled

1. Preheat oven to 180°C.
2. Heat oil, onion and garlic in a pan.
3. Add chops and cook on both sides until golden brown.
4. Mix together the soup, milk, red and green capsicum, mushrooms, tomatoes, Worcestershire sauce, soy sauce, basil, salt and pepper.
5. Place chops and new potatoes in an ovenproof dish, pour over the soup mixture and bake in the oven, uncovered, for 30 minutes, or until tender.

SERVES EIGHT

Cloud Valley

This is a simple recipe, which I cook for the family in the country. It's hearty, nourishing and really tasty. I hope you enjoy it too.

JOHN LAWS, BROADCASTER

Farm Pie

- 8 medium new potatoes
- 1 tablespoon olive oil
- 1 tablespoon butter, plus extra
- 3 onions, finely chopped
- 1½kg minced beef
- salt and pepper
- 3 tablespoons Worcestershire sauce
- rind of 1 lemon, grated
- freshly ground nutmeg
- ½ cup (125ml) milk
- 3 tomatoes

1. Preheat oven to 200°C.
2. Wash potatoes and steam in their skins until soft.
3. Heat oil and butter in a large pan and fry the onions until transparent and soft.
4. Add minced meat and stir vigorously. Add salt, pepper, Worcestershire sauce, lemon rind and two good pinches of nutmeg. Simmer gently for 15 minutes, stirring frequently.
5. Pour milk over the steamed potatoes and mash well, adding salt and pepper to taste.
6. Place meat mixture into an ovenproof dish, finely slice tomatoes and place a layer on top of the meat mixture, then cover with the mashed potato. Dot the top of the potato with small dollops of butter.
7. Bake in the oven for approximately half-an-hour (or until the potato is well browned).

SERVES 10

Smoked Salmon

When it comes to kids, be firm, but allow them to run on a loose rein.

Baby Gai

Risotto

- 60g butter
- 1 large onion, chopped
- 1½ cups (350g) arborio rice
- ½ cup (125ml) dry white wine
- 3 cups (750ml) chicken stock
- 1 bunch asparagus, cut into small pieces
- ¾ cup (150g) sliced button mushrooms
- ¾ cup (150g) smoked salmon pieces
- 2–3 tablespoons light sour cream
- 2–3 tablespoons lemon juice
- salt and pepper

1 • Heat butter in a large microwave-proof bowl on high for one minute.
2 • Add onion and cook for two minutes.
3 • Stir in the rice and cook for one minute.
4 • Add wine and cook for one minute.
5 • Add stock and cook, covered with cling wrap, for 16 minutes.
6 • Add asparagus and mushrooms, stir through, and cook for a final five minutes.
7 • Carefully stir through the salmon, sour cream, lemon juice, salt and pepper. Leave to rest for a couple of minutes. Meanwhile, get the kids to set the table and make a simple salad.
8 • Voila! Dinner is served — now who is on washing-up duty tonight?

SERVES FOUR

Lemon Tarragon

Balancing a busy career and a family is a real challenge; I've had to accept that I can't be 'superwoman' all the time. I try to constantly examine my priorities and my needs—everything else has to come a long way after family and work. If that means we eat pasta and microwave the vegies, then fine!

Simone's daughters Yvann and Lucienne

SIMONE YOUNG, CONDUCTOR

Chicken

- 1 tablespoon butter, plus an extra knob
- 1 tablespoon ground tarragon
- 1 whole chicken
- 1 lemon, cut into eight pieces
- salt and pepper
- 1 tablespoon olive oil
- 2 tablespoons water

1. Preheat oven to 220°C.
2. Mash together the softened butter and half the ground tarragon.
3. With a spoon (or a finger!) make a space between the skin and the meat over both breasts of the chicken. (You need to attack from the neck cavity and push through the thin layer of fat/membrane under the skin. Once you've shown them how, the kids usually enjoy doing this bit too!)
4. Fill the spaces between the skin and the meat with the butter and tarragon mixture.
5. Stuff the chicken with lemon pieces, a knob of butter and the remaining tarragon. Season with salt and pepper.
6. Secure the openings with skewers or string and put the chicken on a grill stand in a baking pan.
7. Pour the olive oil and water into the pan and cover the whole pan with foil. Place in the oven and bake according to the weight of the chicken (approximately one hour for an average-sized chicken) and remove the foil about half-an-hour before it's cooked.
8. Serve with roast vegies, tagliatelle, steamed broccoli and gravy.

 SERVES SIX

Hamburgers with

There is nothing your kids could ever do that would stop you loving them.

Hamburgers
- 500g lean minced beef
- 1 onion, finely chopped
- 1 egg, lightly beaten
- 1/3 cup (20g) fresh breadcrumbs
- 2 tablespoons tomato sauce
- 1 teaspoon steak seasoning
- salt and pepper

The Works
- 1/4 cup (45g) butter
- 2 onions, cut into thin rings
- 4 eggs
- 4 rashers rindless bacon, halved
- 4 large hamburger buns, halved
- shredded lettuce
- 1 large tomato, sliced
- 4 large beetroot slices, drained
- 4 pineapple rings, drained
- 4 slices cheddar cheese, halved
- tomato sauce, for serving

the Works

1 • Place hamburger ingredients in a large bowl. Use your hands to mix well.
2 • Divide mixture into four portions and shape into round burgers.
3 • Heat a frying pan or barbecue grill and brush lightly with oil. Cook burgers for three to four minutes each side, or until cooked through.
4 • While the burgers are cooking, heat the butter in another frying pan, add onion rings and cook over medium heat until brown. Remove and keep warm.
5 • Fry eggs and bacon separately in the frying pan.
6 • Toast buns and top each one with lettuce, tomato, beetroot and pineapple. Add a meat burger and a cheese slice and finish with some onion, egg and bacon. Serve with tomato sauce on the side.

SERVES FOUR

Barbecued Steamed Fish

*This is so simple yet flavoursome—
you will never eat fish any other way again!*

- juice of 1 lemon
- 1 onion, chopped
- 1 capsicum, chopped
- sprinkle of Thai dressing
- splash coconut milk
- salt and pepper
- 1 whole fish, or fish fillets, e.g. ling, perch or trout

1. Combine onion, capsicum, coconut milk, Thai dressing and lemon juice in a bowl and season with salt and pepper.
2. Put the fish on a piece of aluminium foil, pour over the sauce and wrap the foil around the fish, sealing it tightly so the juice can't escape.
3. Cook fish in the foil on the barbecue, for 10 minutes on each side.
4. Serve immediately with fresh salad and garlic bread.

SERVES TWO

MARK TAYLOR, FORMER TEST CRICKET CAPTAIN

something sweet

My Nanna Coy's

I was taught this recipe by my grandmother, Nanna Coy. She used to come round to our house in Chatswood every Saturday afternoon to cook these delicious butterfly cakes. My three sisters and I were more than happy to help in the kitchen, especially when it was time to fill the cakes with jam and cream. So, as a mother of two, I could think of nothing better to feed my children. They are just so quick and easy to make—but I warn you, they never last long with children around!

★

KERRY CHIKAROVSKI, POLITICIAN

Butterfly Cakes

- 1 ½ cups (185g) self-raising flour
- 1 cup (240g) caster sugar
- 125g butter, softened
- 3 eggs
- ¼ cup (60ml) milk
- 1 teaspoon vanilla essence
- ½ cup (125g) jam
- 1¼ cups (300ml) carton thickened cream, whipped

1. Preheat oven to 200°C.
2. Sift flour and sugar into an electric mixer bowl. Add butter, eggs, milk and vanilla essence and beat on medium speed for three minutes until mixture is smooth and light in colour. (You can also do this by hand if you prefer.)
3. Divide cake mixture between 12 prepared paper cases.
4. Bake in the oven for 20 minutes until lightly browned. Leave to cool on a wire rack. Using a fine pointed knife, cut a circle out of the top of each cake and cut each circle in half.
5. Fill each cake with ½ teaspoon jam and top with whipped cream.
6. Place half circles back on top of cakes in the form of butterfly wings, sift icing sugar over cakes and serve immediately.

MAKES 12 CAKES

Maureen's Very

The best thing a woman can do for her children is to love their father...

Maureen with her son Patrick

Easy Meringues

- 5 egg whites
- pinch salt
- 1½ cups (360g) caster sugar

1. Beat egg whites with salt until soft peaks form.
2. Continue beating, adding 1 tablespoon caster sugar at a time until all the sugar is dissolved.
3. Using two spoons, place rounded heaps of the mixture on a lightly greased tray and bake in the oven at 100°C for 2 hours.
4. Turn off the oven and allow meringues to cool inside oven.

MAKES 12 MERINGUES

Julian's Grand

I can only cook one of these at a time so there is some control over the flow of maple syrup. It also means that I can cater for the different wishes of my five children as to the size and shape of the pancake—one in the shape of an Aussie football is fine, but I have yet to master a Giotto-like circle! The best thing is that it gives me a chance to communicate with the children individually as they hover expectantly around the stove.

- 1½ cups (185g) self-raising flour
- 1 teaspoon baking powder
- 2 tablespoons caster sugar
- pinch of salt
- 2 eggs, lightly beaten
- 1 cup (250ml) milk
- 60g butter, melted, plus extra for the pan
- maple syrup, to serve
- Greek yoghurt, to serve

JULIAN GAVIN, OPERA SINGER

Hotcakes

1. Sift flour, baking powder, sugar and salt into a mixing bowl and make a well in the centre.
2. Pour eggs, milk and melted butter into the well. Using a wire whisk, beat in a frenzied fashion until all the liquid is incorporated and the batter is smooth and free of lumps. (You are supposed to leave the batter, covered, to rest for 20 minutes or so, but I have found that in practice the needs of the starving multitude demand an immediate launch into the next stage of proceedings!)
3. Melt a little butter in a frying pan, pour in about $1/4$ cup pancake mixture and swirl around to make the shape of your choice.
4. Cook for about one minute over a medium heat, until the under side is golden and there are some encouraging bubbles on the visible side.
5. Turn over and cook on the other side briefly. (When you get really good and you know that they are not going to disintegrate as you turn them, try impressing your kids by flipping them over with a petulant flick of the wrist—careful, not too high!).
6. Repeat the process, greasing the pan between each hotcake.
7. When you've perfected them, the hotcakes should taste light and fluffy and go superbly with a dollop of good Greek yoghurt on the side and copious amounts of maple syrup. They are best eaten immediately, although in our house the idea of that not happening is ludicrous!

MAKES SIX HOTCAKES

Betty Farrelly's

We made it a rule that every Sunday the family spent the day together, even when my three daughters were teenagers. We'd go surfing, skiing or sailboarding, but the main thing was that we were together.

Midget aged fourteen

Dried Fruit Pie

- 1½ cups (250g) currants
- 1½ cups (250g) raisins
- 1 tablespoon cornflour
- 2 tablespoons honey
- 185g butter
- 2 cups (250g) wholemeal flour
- 3 tablespoons golden syrup
- 1 egg, beaten

1 • Preheat oven to 130°C.
2 • Place raisins and currants in a saucepan, cover with water and boil for 20 minutes.
3 • Mix cornflour with a little water and add to currants and raisins, stirring to thicken the mixture. Stir in the honey.
4 • Knead butter into the flour, add a little water and mix well, then add golden syrup.
5 • Divide pastry into two parts, and roll out to form base and lid of pie.
6 • Line a greased baking dish with pastry and pour fruit mixture on top.
7 • Cover with pastry lid, glaze with beaten egg and bake in the oven for half-an-hour.
8 • This is best consumed with cream or ice-cream—or both!

SERVES SIX

Peanut Butter Biscuits

These are my daughters' favourite biscuits!

- ½ cup (90g) butter
- ½ cup (120g) white sugar
- ¾ cup (135g) brown sugar
- ½ teaspoon vanilla essence
- 1 egg
- ½ cup (125g) peanut butter
- 1½ cups (185g) plain flour
- 1 teaspoon bicarbonate of soda
- pinch salt

1. Preheat oven to 190°C.
2. Soften butter, add sugar and beat until creamy.
3. Add vanilla essence and egg, beat well and stir in peanut butter.
4. Sift flour, bicarbonate of soda and salt into the mixture and combine until smooth.
5. Press mixture into a prepared baking tray and bake in the oven for 15 minutes.
6. When cooked, cut into slices while still warm.

MAKES 12 BISCUITS

GILLIAN ARMSTRONG, FILM DIRECTOR

Perfect Pecan Pie

The best advice I could give any parent is to be a good listener.

- 3 eggs
- 1 cup (180g) light brown sugar
- 1 cup (250ml) light Karo syrup (corn syrup)
- 125g butter, melted
- 1 teaspoon vanilla
- 1 cup (180g) pecans
- 1 unbaked 20cm pie shell

1. Preheat oven to 170°C.
2. Beat eggs in a large bowl, then add sugar and Karo syrup. Mix well.
3. Add melted butter, vanilla and pecans and stir to combine.
4. Pour mixture into pie shell and bake in the oven for approximately one hour, or until the centre is firm.
5. Serve with cream or ice-cream.

 SERVES SIX

WIMBLEDON CHAMPION, JOHN NEWCOMBE

Mother's Garden

This recipe is from my mother, who cooked this dessert using the fruit from our very large garden. We were often asked to go and collect the strawberries, but only my father was allowed to pick the rhubarb as he used a sharp knife to cut the stalk. It smelled beautiful while baking and was made in a large batch to last a few days.

★

SERGE DANSEREAU, CHEF

Fruit Crumble

- 2 bunches fresh rhubarb
- 4 punnets fresh strawberries
- ½ cup (120g) white sugar
- 1 tablespoon cornflour
- 1 cup (125g) plain flour
- 1 cup (180g) butter
- 1 cup (220g) oatmeal
- 1 cup (180g) brown sugar

1. Preheat oven to 170°C.
2. Trim rhubarb of any green leaves and peel off fibrous part of root. Cut into 3cm-long pieces.
3. Wash and hull strawberries, and cut in half.
4. In a bowl mix white sugar, cornflour and strawberries and rhubarb. Put in a large, deep ovenproof dish.
5. Make a crumble by mixing the flour, butter, oatmeal and brown sugar by hand or with a pastry whisk, allowing the mixture to remain fairly chunky.
6. Spread mixture on top of fruit and bake for 25 minutes or until rhubarb is cooked.
7. Serve with vanilla ice-cream.

SERVES 12

Very Sticky Date

I'm absolutely certain that the worst things for you to eat are definitely the yummiest. This one is wickedly high in fat and sugar, yet it's worth every mouthful. It's easy to make and everyone will love it. Go on—give it a try. Don't deny yourself. You only live once so at least make it enjoyable. This recipe has been one of my favourites for twenty-odd years and I'm sure it'll still be a favourite for many years to come.

Johanna aged fifteen

JOHANNA GRIGGS, SWIMMER AND TELEVISION PERSONALITY

Pudding

- ¾ cup (180g) dates, stoned and chopped as finely as desired
- 1 teaspoon bicarbonate of soda
- 1¼ cups (300ml) boiling water
- 60g butter
- ¾ cup (180g) caster sugar
- 2 eggs
- 1½ cups (185g) self-raising flour
- 1 teaspoon vanilla essence

Sauce
- 1¼ cups (300ml) thickened cream
- 2 cups (360g) brown sugar
- 1¼ cups (225g) butter

1. Preheat oven to 180°C.
2. Grease an 18cm square cake tin with butter, then dust with flour.
3. In a bowl, mix dates and bicarbonate of soda. Pour boiling water over the top and leave to stand. The dates will soften and expand while you prepare rest of mix.
4. Cream together butter and sugar, then add eggs. Beat well. Fold flour in gradually.
5. Add date mixture and vanilla essence to cake mixture, stir well and pour into the cake tin.
6. Bake in the oven for 30–40 minutes, until cooked.
7. Place the sauce ingredients into a saucepan and bring to the boil. Reduce heat and simmer for five minutes.
8. Pour sauce over the pudding and serve with ice-cream.

Serves six

Golden Puffed

My favourite recipe is golden puffed dumplings. The taste is exquisite and highly recommended! I first had them while on a ski touring expedition in 1966 at Albina Hutte, on the Kosciuszko mountain range.

Dick aged five

Dumplings

Dumplings
- 1 cup (125g) self-raising flour
- pinch salt
- 1 tablespoon butter
- 2 tablespoons milk
- 1 egg

Syrup
- 1 cup (250ml) water
- 1 tablespoon butter
- ½ cup (120g) sugar
- 2 tablespoons golden syrup

1. Sift flour and salt into a bowl and rub the butter in well with your fingertips, until mixture resembles breadcrumbs.
2. Combine milk and egg.
3. Make a well in the centre of the mixture and add combined milk and egg. Stir well to form a soft dough. Divide the mixture into little balls.
4. To make the syrup, place water, butter, sugar and golden syrup in a deep saucepan and stir over a medium heat until sugar is dissolved.
5. Gently drop balls into saucepan, cover and simmer for 20 minutes.
6. Serve with custard.

 SERVES FOUR

Monica's Mum's

My favourite cookie recipe is a shortbread recipe my mum taught me when I was about 10. It's fantastic with a very cold glass of milk. The only practical tip I'd give is to make sure you hide the cookie tin once you've baked them because whoever has a piece can never stop at just one—it's scrumptious!

Monica aged five

Shortbread

- 1 cup (180g) butter
- 1 cup (240g) caster sugar
- ½ teaspoon vanilla essence
- finely grated rind of 1 orange or lemon
- 2 cups (250g) plain flour

1. Preheat oven to 180°C. Line a 20cm square tray with baking paper.
2. Cream butter and sugar together in a small mixing bowl. Add vanilla essence and orange or lemon rind and beat for one minute. Fold in the flour and stir until the mixture is combined.
3. Spread into prepared tray, and smooth over with a spatula.
4. Bake in the oven for about 15 minutes until golden.
5. Slice into diamond shapes and dust with icing sugar.

MAKES 40 BISCUITS

Nutty Chocolate

I've never pushed my love of surfing onto my kids, but they both have fun in the waves.

Mark with his son Max and daughter Holly

MARK WARREN, WORLD SURFING CHAMPION

Brownies

- 125g butter, melted
- 1 cup (180g) brown sugar
- 1 teaspoon vanilla essence
- 4 eggs, lightly beaten
- 3/4 cup (125g) chopped chocolate
- 3/4 cup (125g) chopped macadamias
- 1 cup (125g) self-raising flour
- cocoa powder to serve

1. Preheat oven to moderate 180°C. Line a 20cm square cake tin with baking paper.
2. Mix together butter, sugar and vanilla. Add eggs and stir to combine. Stir in chocolate and macadamias.
3. Add flour and mix well.
4. Spoon mixture into prepared tin and bake for 40–50 minutes.
5. Remove the tin from the oven and stand on a wire rack to cool.
6. Dust with cocoa powder and cut into squares just before serving.

MAKES 16 BROWNIES

Colourful Toffee

Toffee apples were my favourite treat as a child, and my own children are now carrying on the family tradition...without realising how healthy they actually are! When we cook these, looking down on us from the kitchen wall is a creed both my husband and I grew up with, by Dorothy Law Nolte, and one we try, as parents, to live by:

If children live with criticism, they learn to condemn.
If children live with hostility, they learn to fight.
If children live with ridicule, they learn to feel shy.
If children live with shame, they learn to feel guilty.
If children live with encouragement, they learn confidence.
If children live with tolerance, they learn patience.
If children live with praise, they learn appreciation.
If children live with acceptance, they learn to love.
If children live with approval, they learn to like themselves.
If children live with sharing, they learn generosity.
If children live with honesty, they learn truthfulness.
If children live with kindness and consideration, they learn respect.
If children live with security, they learn to have faith in themselves and in those about them.
If children live with friendliness, they learn the world is a nice place in which to live.

Apple Treats

- 1 cup (240g) sugar
- ¼ cup (60ml) water
- 1 teaspoon vinegar
- pinch cream of tartar
- a few drops of food colouring of your choice
- 6 Granny Smith apples
- wooden skewers

1. Stir sugar, water, vinegar and cream of tartar in a saucepan over low heat until sugar dissolves.
2. Bring to boil without stirring and cook until toffee starts to turn golden.
3. Remove from heat. To test, drip a toffee blob into cold water —if it sets, it's ready. Add food colouring.
4. Insert skewers into apples, then swirl apples in toffee. Place on a greased tray to set.

MAKES SIX TOFFEE APPLES

Lisa aged ten

Fruit Dessert for

When I was a boy, I dreamed a lot about all different things—adventure, sport, people, things to do, ambitions...I still dream a lot! Never lose the ability to dream.

This is my favourite dish because I can make it myself, it's colourful with many different textures, it's low in fat and I can have it for breakfast with cereal or as a dessert with my favourite Greek-style plain yoghurt. Ice-cream is delicious too.

JOHN BERTRAND, AMERICA'S CUP CHAMPION

the Family

- 6–8 whole, firm fruits in season, e.g. peaches, plums and nectarines
- ½ cup (90g) Muscovite, molasses or dark brown sugar
- 1 cup (250ml) water
- 1 lemon, cut into quarters
- 1 tablespoon nuts, linseed or sunflower seeds
- 3–4 stalks of mint (optional)

1. Wash fruit and put in a saucepan. Sprinkle sugar over fruit, add water and lemon quarters, giving the lemons a bit of a squeeze as you drop them in, and cover with a lid.
2. Cook over a medium heat for about five minutes then gently check with a fork that fruit is soft.
3. Turn off the heat and leave to cool.
4. To serve, place fruit in your favourite bowl, pour over the liquid, add some nuts, serve with yoghurt or ice-cream, garnish with mint and dig in!

SERVES FOUR

Fruit Bread and

Parenting is a two-way street—parents learn as much from their kids as kids do from parents. Each child is different from their siblings, with each requiring their own unique approach for effective parenting. Just remember, the perfect parent is yet to be born!

Butter Custard

- 6 slices healthy bread
- margarine, or butter, to spread
- 2 ripe bananas or ½ cup (150g) sultanas (or both)
- 2 eggs
- 3 cups (750ml) milk (or soy milk, or milk substitute)
- 1 teaspoon vanilla essence
- 2 tablespoons brown sugar
- 1 tablespoon jam, any flavour

1. Preheat oven to 190°C.
2. Lightly spread the bread with margarine or butter and cut into 3cm squares.
3. Layer bread and sliced bananas or sultanas (or both) in a baking dish.
4. Mix together eggs, milk, vanilla and brown sugar. Pour over the bread and fruit and allow to stand for 10–15 minutes to absorb the liquid.
5. Place small dollops of your favourite jam on top.
6. Bake in the oven until golden brown and set (approximately 45 minutes).
7. Serve warm with cream, ice-cream or fruit.

 SERVES EIGHT

STEPHANIE HUTCHINSON, COMPILER OF JUST EAT!

Eily's Chocolate

For every birthday or celebration, my mother would bake this cake. It is only now that I know why—it is so quick and easy to make, yet tastes great. Now my children, Georgia and Hal, make it with me, licking the spoon and bowl when finished. It is especially good with chocolate icing, strawberries and cream, or sprinkled with desiccated coconut.

Stephanie's daughter Georgia

Cake

- 3 tablespoons melted butter
- 1 cup (125g) self-raising flour
- ½ cup (125ml) milk
- 1 teaspoon vanilla essence
- 3 tablespoons cocoa
- 1 cup (240g) sugar
- 2 eggs

1 • Preheat oven to 170°C.
2 • Place all ingredients in an electric mixer and blend for one minute.
3 • Pour into a prepared cake tin and bake in the oven for 30 minutes, or until cooked.

SERVES SIX TO EIGHT

Index

bacon 27
beans 19, 39
beef 39, 41, 44, 49, 56, 61, 63, 75, 80
biscuits 92
brownies 103
butterfly cakes 85

casserole 39
cauliflower 43
cheese 11, 35, 43, 55, 69
chicken 50, 55, 69, 70, 79
chocolate 103
chocolate cake 111
custard 109

damper 30
desserts 85–111
dried fruit pie 91
dumplings 99

eggs 22, 26

fish 46, 53, 67, 82
fried rice 37
fritters 11
fruit bread 109
fruit crumble 95
fruit dessert 107

ginger shallots 47
gravy 45

hamburgers 80
hotcakes 89

john dory 47

lamb 9, 73
lemon 79
lentils 21

macaroni 35
meatballs 49, 65
meatloaf 66
meringues 87
mushroom 32

olives 67

pasta 35, 41, 53, 69
pasties 58
peas 12
pecan pie 93
pies 63, 70, 75, 91, 93
pizza 14
potato 11, 12, 43
pumpkin 17

quiche 33

rissoles 44
risotto 77

schnitzel 50
shepherd's pie 63
shortbread 101
smoked salmon 77
soup 9, 12, 17, 21
spaghetti 41
spinach 33
spring rolls 24
sticky date pudding 97

tarragon 79
toffee apples 105
tomato sauce 49, 65, 73
tomatoes 14, 55
tuna 53

vegetables 9, 10, 12, 17, 19, 43, 44, 61, 70

zucchini 11

First published in Australia in 2001 by
New Holland Publishers (Australia) Pty Ltd
Sydney • Auckland • London • Cape Town

14 Aquatic Drive Frenchs Forest NSW 2086 Australia
218 Lake Road Northcote Auckland New Zealand
24 Nutford Place London W1H 5DQ United Kingdom
80 McKenzie Street Cape Town 8001 South Africa

Copyright © 2001 in text: K-L Clinton and Stephanie Hutchinson
Copyright © 2001 in photographs as credited below
Copyright © 2001 in illustrations: Luisa Laino
Copyright © 2001 New Holland Publishers (Australia) Pty Ltd

All rights reserved. No part of this publication may be reproduced, stored in a retrieval system or transmitted, in any form or by any means, electronic, mechanical, photocopying, recording or otherwise, without the prior written permission of the publishers and copyright holders.

National Library of Australia Cataloguing-in-Publication Data:

Just eat! famous Aussies get kids into the kitchen.

Includes index.
ISBN 1 86436 710 5

1. Cookery, Australian. I. Clinton, K-L. II. Hutchinson, Stephanie. III. Title.
641.5994

Publisher: Averill Chase
Project Editor: Sophie Church
Designer: Peta Nugent
Design Assistant: Jenny Mansfield
Cover design: Peta Zoubakin
Illustrations: Luisa Laino
Reproduction: Pica
Printed by South China Press

This book is typeset in Meta Plus Book 13pt.

Photographic acknowledgements:
David Atkins: p.8; Nicky Buckley: p.10; K-L Clinton: p.28; Alyssa-Jane Cook: p.32; Greg Doyle: p.46; Maureen Duval: p.86; Midget Farrelly: p.90; Jeff Fenech: p. 48; Tim Fischer: p.64; Richard Glover: p.13; Belinda Green: p.16; Johanna Griggs: p.96; Wendy Heather Hunter: p.52; Stephanie Hutchinson: p.110; Helen Kaminski: p.57; Antonia Kidman: p.20; Gretel Killeen: p.36; Elle Macpherson: p.60; Iain Murray: p.68; Rebel Penfold-Russell: p.42; Nova Peris-Kneebone: p.40; Anne Sargeant: p.72; Joanna Savill: p.23; Dick Smith: p.98; Monica Trapaga: p.100; Mark Warren: p.102; Gai Waterhouse: p.76; Lisa Wilkinson: p.105; Simone Young: p.78; back cover flap: K-L Clinton and Stephanie Hutchinson.

Poem on p.104 adapted from the book *Children Learn What They Live*, Copyright © 1998 by Dorothy Law Nolte and Rachel Harris. The poem 'Children Learn What They Live' on p.vi Copyright © 1972 by Dorothy Law Nolte. Used by permission of Workman Publishing Co., Inc., New York. All rights reserved.